AF419209

TOM HENRICKSEN

Musings of a Developer

A collection of popular posts

Copyright © 2024 by Tom Henricksen

All rights reserved. No part of this publication may be reproduced, stored or transmitted in any form or by any means, electronic, mechanical, photocopying, recording, scanning, or otherwise without written permission from the publisher. It is illegal to copy this book, post it to a website, or distribute it by any other means without permission.

First edition

This book was professionally typeset on Reedsy.
Find out more at reedsy.com

Contents

Preface

This is a collection of popular blog posts I have shared over the past years. As a developer, I enjoy digging into topics that catch my eye. From code to interpersonal collaboration, it is fun to explore these ideas.

While my job can be quite technical we all must work on teams. That is where our true leverage lies. As an individual, we can only achieve so much. Even though many developers are introverts we must overcome our inclination.

Enjoy this collection and please reach out with questions or topics that you would enjoy reading about!

1

Make a technical career shift: from Developer to DevOps right now!

As more companies switch to DevOps more developers want to make the switch. What skills do you need to make this career transition from developer to DevOps? How can we go about starting this change? If you want to make this change you are in the right spot!

I have gone through a similar transition in my career. From being a developer to working on DevOps teams it can be a bit of a change. There are a few skills and mindset shifts we need to go through to be successful.

As a quick disclaimer, each company may have a different DevOps stack and practices. We will cover some of the more common and basic skills needed.

Cloud

Even people outside of technology hear the constant talk about cloud technologies. Mark Henke shared, "So what does it take to become a successful DevOps engineer?...

The first skill set we'll cover is the ability to leverage cloud and serverless platforms." It is pretty critical to know how to use these technologies for a DevOps role.

Henke continues, "To be a DevOps engineer, it is and will continue to be key to understanding these cloud offerings." So I guess cloud isn't a fad after all!

Depending on the organization you are with you will need to understand their particular cloud provider. Most companies use Amazon but, there are other players out there.

Linux

To be a successful DevOps Engineer you need to know your way around the command line. Linux is a tool that is in use in most DevOps shops. Igor Kantor points out, "Honestly, the best way to do it is to just install Linux (Fedora or Ubuntu) at home and use that as much as you can.

You will break things, you will get stuck and then you will have to fix it all and in the process, you will learn Linux!" So you can do that next weekend.

Continuous

The holy grail for many DevOps shops is to get to continuous deployments. I just want to say not every shop will get there right away. It depends on many factors. That is why I think it is best to focus on continuous integration.

Authors Jez Humble and David Fowler talk about the **deployment pipeline** in their book Continuous Delivery(affiliate link). The deployment pipeline is really taking the idea of continuous integration to the next level. Add to it so deployments are seamless and quicker.

Configuration Management

Version Control is a critical part of the DevOps lifecycle. We need to be ready to roll back our changes quickly to avert disaster. Distributed version control systems like Git have been invaluable for many DevOps teams. It can be the heart of a deployment pipeline.

As an experienced Java developer, I know that managing dependencies is equally important. There are many tools to use for this purpose depending on your codebase. Application configuration needs to be seamless as well. This is a good point to make the DevOps team collaborate between developers and operations.

Build

There are a lot of options out there to build tools. As a Java developer, I have mainly used Ant and Maven. Of course, there is NAnt, Rake, Buildr, or good ole' Make. So depending on what works best for you but you have to choose one.

Jez and David recommend a few principles and practices for Continuous Delivery. Create a script for each stage of your deployment pipeline. This can be helpful to break it up and then modify it as necessary.

Use the same script to deploy in every environment. That way there are no surprises when you go to production!

Monitoring

In the old world, developers would throw code over the wall and let the operations team monitor it. DevOps eliminates that hand off as it is all one team.

Gary Gruver points out in his book Starting and Scaling DevOps in the Enterprise,(affiliate link) "Frequently, the first place in the DP(Deployment Pipeline) that monitoring is used is in production. This is problematic because when the code is released to customers, developers haven't been able to see potential problems clearly before the customer experience highlights it."

DevOps teams must have monitoring from the start. We can get eyes on any memory leaks or database issues before we deploy it to our Quality Assurance team. Therefore, we can fix issues before we get into a new environment.

In conclusion, the move from developer to DevOps is not impossible. It just takes time to add some skills you need to be productive. If you have previous experience with some of these it can be helpful.

What skills did I miss?

2

Building A Great Tech Team

"Coming together is a beginning. Keeping together is progress. Working together is success."
Henry Ford

Recruiting the right people is not an easy task. Top technical talent essentially has their pick. Companies try to bring in good people but, a few duds will sneak in. Hiring a new person can be tough on so many levels. We can ask them behavioral questions. Grill them over particular technologies. Still, we can end up with the wrong person. Part of the issue is we get in a hurry to bring new people in. To have the right person we need to slow down and take our time. "But the good people will be gone!" That may be but, hiring the wrong person can be very expensive. It can also ruin a good team.

Culture Fit

A truly great team is not a group of rock stars. A great team knows how to work together and play their respective roles. Recently in "March Madness" or the Men's NCAA Basketball tournament, there was a Cinderella team that made it to the Final Four. Loyola University of Chicago's team beat many higher-ranked teams to get to the Final Four. These players were not all top recruits but, they played well together.

Similar things happen with great tech teams. When you have a good culture and talented people who want to work together it raises the bar. Each member helps push the other team members. They learn from each other and respect each other's opinions. Organizations that establish the culture and know what they are looking for can find the right pieces. Organizations that hire flashy candidates too quickly can wind up with some poor fits.

One bad teammate can sour a team quickly. I worked with Cindy (not her real name) for a short while. On her first day, I went to lunch with her and she complained about a few things. I have to admit that raised a flag for me. On your first day, you think it would be all positive. Cindy was hard on her teammates and customers. After a short stay, she was let go. Talent is nice but, you don't want to hire talented-jerks!

Holding Out

We can get in a hurry. "We need someone yesterday!" At times maybe you have even thought, "Someone is better than no one." As I spoke about Cindy before remember one bad hire can have a net negative impact. Working with developers for many years one bad one can create a mess in a hurry. It is best to wait and hold out for the right person.

Dave Ramsey and his organization are notoriously slow in hiring. On their podcast, EntreLeadership they detail the numerous rounds of interviews they send people through. Only if you want to work for him will you stick it out. I would recommend your organization create a process and fine-tune it. If you find a crazy one gets through, it is time to change the process.

Holding out for the right talent

Seed, Feed, and Weed

So you have done all of the previous steps. Now you're done, right? Wrong! Once you have your great team you still have some work to do. Seed. You need to constantly be on the lookout for new people. You might need to grow your team or someone may leave. Feed. Develop the people you have. Get them the coaching and training they need. Perhaps one of them will replace you someday. Weed. People can fool you in the hiring process. Or some people will change. They can become negative or no longer be a good fit. Move them out with care.

3

What is the project status? Red Amber Green what does that mean?

Photo by Scott Warman on Unsplash

Why are these 3 words so hard to say?

"I don't know."

My wife asked me about RAG Status. "What is RAG status used for?"

"Ah.." was about all I had.

It's okay to say those three words.

RAG Status

RAG Status or Red Amber Green is used to communicate project status quickly. It is used to evaluate Key Performance Indicators or KPIs.

The three colors are similar to a traffic light. This is to create a simple reminder of where a project is currently.

Red

Red status means the project is likely to fail. To paraphrase Arthur Miller, **"Attention should be paid to this project!"**

Things are not proceeding. Intervention is needed. Additional resources may be required.

The red status is a bullseye. Managers and stakeholders will ask questions. *They should be seriously concerned.*

Amber

While not as bad as red, amber means we are slightly off course. Stakeholders should keep their eye on this.

For instance, there might be roadblocks in the way. Maybe a key resource just went out on maternity leave.

Corrective action taken here can bring things back on track. *If left alone this project could quickly move to red.*

Green

The green status means all systems are sound. We are moving along as expected.

We wish all projects were green. Although, we know that is not how things always work.

This is the ideal state. Understand that it can be difficult to keep a project always in green. If it is always green you may become suspicious.

Define Terms

When you use terms like this make sure you agree on what they mean.

> It is very important for an organization to be able to understand the trust what status is being reported for a project. Therefore, it is very important to have clearly defined criteria for selecting the correct RAG status. (from PM Majik).

When an organization agrees on the terms then this can be a valuable reporting tool. **If not this can become useless.**

Disadvantages

It can be nice to have a tool like this for a glance. Of course, if people don't honor the agreement they could alter the report. This is a big disadvantage.

Another is that simple indicators may only tell part of the story. For instance, in the complex world of project management, many factors could be at play.

This article points out how we can tend to be too optimistic. "project managers have then is a tendency to play safe and report project is green when in fact it should be amber or red."

The optimism bias can lead us to believe things will work out. When in fact things could be heading south. If we took time and got the help we may be able to save the project.

Advantages

This can be a helpful tool to quickly communicate status. For instance, executives need to quickly see progress. RAG Status can help them briefly review.

In an organization with high trust, this will work. If you find a lack of psychological safety then there will be gamesmanship. Especially if bonuses may be tied to outcomes.

In summary, the RAG status can be helpful. Although it may not always convey the true status. As we discussed this is one data point. Consider using this in conjunction with other information.

4

How to Successfully jump into a new Codebase

Learning a new codebase can be a real challenge. In other words, you have a plan to be successful. This is part of the onboarding process that we have spoken about before. Let's take a few minutes to review some helpful strategies to get you started.

I recently started a new position and it reminded me how important it is for a developer to get acquainted with a codebase. However, codebases are like families. There is no perfect family or codebase. They are all dysfunctional in their way.

No two are alike and each is organized differently. If only there was a treasure map to tell you where things are. Like most developers, I learn by digging in and doing things. Here are a few tips that I have learned along the way.

Mentor

Find a mentor who can guide you through the code. This can shine a light on the key parts. Mattias Petter Johansson says, "Find a programmer already familiar with the code base, and ask them if they are willing to be interrupted a lot during the coming weeks to help answer your silly questions."

Break

This is my personal favorite. Change some code and run the application. Once you break something and see the result try and fix it. Give yourself some time before you call in help. Remember to use your version control to get yourself out of a jam!

Walk

I find it helpful when I am out of town to walk the neighborhood. Similarly, we can walk through the codebase. See how the code is laid out.

If there are a few projects you can look at see if you notice any patterns. That way you can know where the tests are and the code is. Open up the files and see how they are set up. Does each file have a unique purpose? What do the methods look like?

Why?

Technologists focus on technology. The organization is the main focus, not the technology. Think about why this application exists. Ask better questions to get a better understanding.

Read

Read and review any documentation they give you. Sometimes the documentation you get is out of date. After that, prepare questions you can go over with someone who can help.

Add

Change the code and create your documentation. Therefore you add to it as you explore and learn. Look for things you might get stuck on often. Follow up with your mentor on these to gain a better understanding.

In conclusion, understanding a codebase takes time. Each time you touch it you become more familiar with it. Build your muscle memory until you feel you have mastered it.

What steps do you take to understand a codebase?
How do you avoid getting lost in a codebase?

5

Object-oriented programming is the world we live in

Early in my technical career, I worked as a programmer in PL/SQL. We developed solutions for many small and medium-sized companies. PL/SQL is a procedural-based programming language. Everything happened inside of a procedure. I was offered to develop in Java and jumped at the chance. I thought it would be easy to develop in an object-oriented programming language.

After a few missteps, I began to realize how different and difficult it could be. That is why I want to take a minute and review some basic principles in object-oriented development. This will help clear up some confusion as you move on.

Object-Oriented Programming

Objects are part of the world we live in. I am writing this on a computer and sitting on a couch. Each of these is an object. In other words, programming with these constructs help us think through and understand the code. Objects are more general and theoretical.

Object-oriented programming allows us to track state and behavior. For instance, our computer could be on or off. The modularity of code is a benefit too. Store information about the object together. Above all, it also allows us to hide information. Our mental model can focus on other things. We can reuse code for similar objects. Then we can replace similar objects and debug the code easily.

Class

Classes have been called the "blueprints" of Java. Once we have them we can create many copies of the object. We have the String class from Java. Using the class constructor we can create many copies.

```
String myString1 = new String("One Class");
String myString2 = new String("Two Class");
```

In this example, we share how we create a few String objects.

```
public class Shoe {
                int size = 1;
                boolean smelly = false;
```

Here is a simple class called Shoe. It has two instance variables to track its size and if it smells.

```
Shoe newShoe = new Shoe();
Shoe oldShoe = new Shoe();
```

We can easily create a few shoe objects. The class or "blueprint" allows us to make as many as we want.

Inheritance

Many of the objects in our world are related. We group things all the time. For instance, we have started with a conversation about shoes. Along with our shoe object, we could create a flip-flop object. This will help us prepare for our upcoming beach vacation.

```
class FlipFlop {
                int size = 1;
                boolean sandy = false;
                }
```

These are both footwear so we could create a parent object. In our Footwear object, we can have a common variable size too.

```
class Footwear {
            int size = 1;
            }
```

Then we can update our Shoe and FlipFlop class to reflect the parent class.

```
class FlipFlop extends Footwear {
            public class Shoe extends Footwear
            {
```

Inheritance helps us group similar qualities in our objects to aid in development. We don't need to start from scratch with each item. We can also reuse functionality as well.

Interface

To drive your car you have a few points of interface. For instance, you can steer with the steering wheel. To speed up we use the accelerator and slow down with the brake. These shield us from the intricacies of the motor and braking system. As developers, we need to shield people from what is behind the interface too.

```
public interface Speed {
            void speedUp();
            void slowDown();
            }
```

Here we have an interface to control speed. We define the interface with two methods to speed up or slow down.

```java
public interface Steering {
            void turnLeft();
            void turnRight();
                }
```

Then to steer we have an interface as well. It allows us to turn to the left and the right.

Behind the scenes, we could have a car that implements these and can do each one.

```java
public class Car implements Speed, Steering {
            @Override
            public void turnLeft() {
                System.out.println("Turn left");
            }                    @Override
            public void turnRight() {
                System.out.println("Turn right");
            }                    @Override
            public void speedUp() {
                System.out.println("Speed up");
            }                    @Override
            public void slowDown() {
                System.out.println("Slow down");
            }                        }
```

As you can see in this simple class we are implementing the interfaces and providing code to do the work.

Package

George Foreman is a famous heavyweight boxer. Oddly he named his five sons George Jr. As you can imagine this could be hard when you are talking in a room full of Georges. Similarly, Java code can have a similar issue if it weren't for packages. Packages are like folders that help us give the code a unique name.

Let's take a look at the String class in Java. It is in the java.lang package. Java gives you access to everything in the java.lang package without having to import anything. In other words, the full name of the String class is java.lang.String.

So if I create a special class for a Tesla car we might put it in a package called com.tesla. So if we use the Car object it would be referred to as the com.tesla.Car. Therefore, we would import it using that full name. Instead of having multiple different Car objects for Honda, Toyota, and Tesla, we can refer to them correctly.

6

The Shockingly Simple Secrets from The Pragmatic Engineer

Photo by krakenimages on Unsplash

I am always on the lookout for excellent developer wisdom. A few months ago a friend recommended checking out the Pragmatic Engineer. Gergely Orosz shares his learnings.

I asked him about his favorite items to share, and he mentioned the following article.

Read

Gergely and I agree on this. Developers must read. "Take the time to read two books per year on software engineering."

That is a nice minimum requirement. Plus there are numerous other things to read about. Networking and databases to name a few.

Learn

I enjoy learning. His next piece of advice got me excited. Gergely shared how we need to learn a language in-depth.

> **Learning the language I used at work in-depth was one of the best decisions I made.** At my first workplace, this was accidental and had to do with the senior developer inspiring me. However, this knowledge became an advantage both at work and when interviewing for other jobs

I did this with my Java skills. We each need to find a level of mastery. For some skills, we can just learn surface-level knowledge. Others require a level of depth.

Refactor

Early in my career, I remember developers talking about refactoring. I wasn't quite sure what that word meant. Then I saw the seminal book Refactoring: Improving Design of Existing Code on a bookshelf.

They define it as *"Refactoring is a controlled technique for improving the design of an existing code base."* I would liken it to the way a chef cleans and organizes their kitchen. It makes the next meal that much easier.

Gergely said how he started doing large refactorings. Then switched to doing smaller ones. Likewise, learning the tools of refactoring too. He said, "I realized I was afraid of refactoring as I missed both the practice and the tools to do this well."

Pair

He also recommends pairing up. Two heads are better than one.

> I feel like pairing is out of style these days. When I started, both Extreme Programming with continuous pairing, TDD, and mob programming were popular things to do. Some of my biggest professional leaps came after pairing with people. These leaps were more significant than reading any book.

As I learn new technologies, pairing is a wonderful way to transfer knowledge.

Teach

My mother was a teacher. She would work with young children to learn the basics. Occasionally, she shared stories of how difficult it was for some to learn.

A few years ago I was allowed to teach mainframe developers how to program in Java. It gave me a greater appreciation for my mother's career. Each student had different challenges.

Gergely learned this wisdom by presenting at conferences. At first, he said he wasn't very good. Each time he would learn and build his skills and understanding.

Every experienced developer I have reached out to shares great suggestions. Gergely Orosz is no different. Keep reading and learning. Once you have built momentum refactor your code and teach others.

7

Software Development from Waterfall to DevOps

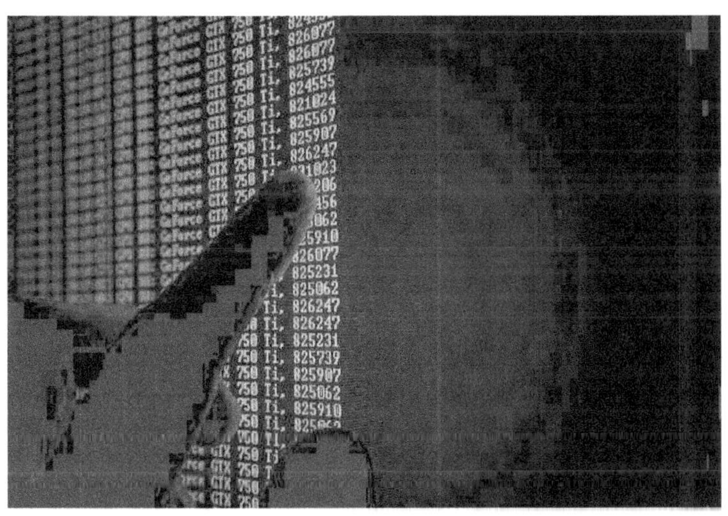

Change is the end result of all true learning.
   Leo Buscaglia

Although as humans we tend to fight change, it happens to us regardless of our attempts. Professionally in software development, I have learned it is better to anticipate change than expect it to stay the same. Doug hoped things would stay the same. He worked at one company doing the same thing for years. Until the company got bought out and technology changed. Doug was found without a job.

Waterfall

I once worked at an organization that tried to have an orderly process to develop software. They had analysts write documentation and then hand it off to developers. Once we completed our work we pushed it to Quality Assurance. This system seemed to make sense. It had one major flaw. More on that later.

The waterfall process or Software Development Life-cycle (SDLC) is composed of six steps. First, we gather requirements for the software. Second, we design the new system followed by implementation. Once complete we have testing and then deployment. The final step is maintenance.

SDLC assumes that we develop everything together, also known as the Big Bang. So we have one release at the end. It follows a gated approach. We gather all the requirements upfront. After that step, there can be no change in the requirements. Therefore, we note the major flaw.

Agile

Many people have tried to define what agile is. I like the definition from Agile in a Nutshell.

> "Agile is a time-boxed, iterative approach to software delivery that builds software incrementally from the start of the project, instead of trying to deliver it all at once near the end."

That hits on many of the key points. Making things time-boxed is a distinction from the SDLC model. It changes the question, "When will it be done?" to "What can we do in two weeks?" Multiple agile approaches use iterations or sprints. Where waterfall just does everything at once with little to no feedback loops.

Agile brings with it a set of distinct benefits. First and foremost is the adaptability. Businesses can gain a strong advantage by being able to quickly react to the changes in the market. In Eric Ries's book The Lean Startup, he discusses the ability to incrementally deliver and get market feedback. Essentially we reduce waste through our iterations. Customers use our new feature and we know we hit the mark. If we hear crickets we know it is not in demand. LinkedIn does this with many of its new enhancements. They slowly turn on the feature to a few people. If it doesn't break and they use it they turn it on to more users. To give back to the Agile community I have created the Agile Online Summit.

DevOps

Many organizations that were trying Agile have moved on to DevOps. This movement has combined two areas to achieve better collaboration. Here is how Wikipedia defines it.

> DevOps is a software development model that com-

bines development and operations together stressing communication, integration, automation, collaboration, and cooperation.

Essentially we want to break down barriers that happen when we hand off work. What could happen when a developer gives some code to be released to the operations staff is balls can be dropped. If we combine those roles we strive to eliminate things.

There are many benefits to DevOps. More frequent deployments are a big one many companies focus on. Continuous Deployment is what a lot will strive for. Along with this, it brings faster time to market. Quality is a focus as well. Creating automated tests to enhance quality helps drive out defects.

8

Staying Above The Line: Drama or Presence

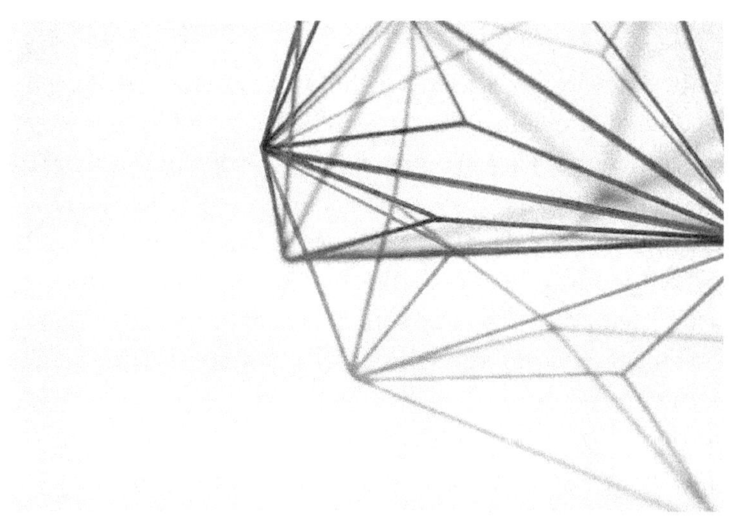

I have been collaborating with Greg Jensen for a while. We presented last fall at Iowa Code Camp and are working together for IBADD too. In a recent discussion, he explained to me the concept of staying above the line from the book The 15 Commitments of Conscious Leadership.

Working from?

The book explains that as conscious leaders we need to understand if we are working from the presence or the drama triangle. Presence is above the line and the drama triangle is below. Where most organizations spend the bulk of their time in the drama triangle. In this people are focused on blame, being right, and fear.

Characters

In the drama triangle, there are three characters. The "Hero" is focused on providing temporary relief and not facing the real issues involved. The next character is the "Villian" who tries to lay blame on others. They use statements like "I should have…" and "It is your fault". The last character in the Drama Triangle is the "Victim". They are dealing with the effects of others that cause their problems. A person, circumstance, or condition is the root of their problem. The victim is powerless in the drama triangle.

Presence

When we move above the line these characters change. The "Victim" becomes the "Creator" and takes responsibility for their lives. The "Villain" becomes the "Challenger" and brings healthy pressure to lead to breakthroughs. Finally, the "Hero" becomes the "Coach" where they empower others to create the outcome they are looking for. Teams working above the line are more aligned and energized.

Statements

Let's examine a few statements to help you understand.

I commit to taking full responsibility for the circumstances of my life at XYZ, and I commit to supporting others to take full responsibility for their lives.

Is this statement above or below the line?

I commit to blaming others and myself for what is wrong at XYZ. I commit to being a victim, villain, or hero and take more or less than 100% responsibility

How about this one?

What do you think about these next two sets of statements?

I commit to growing in self-awareness. I commit to regard every interaction as an opportunity to learn. I commit to curiosity as a path to rapid learning.

I commit to being right and to seeing this situation as something that is happening to me. I commit to being defensive, especially when I am certain I am RIGHT.

Does there seem to be different tones in each one?

When you find yourself stressed try this approach out.

Breathe, Pause, and Shift Be aware that you have drifted below the line and commit to leading and interacting with others from a place of openness

9

Check out what to put in your developer scorecard

Photo by Courtney Cook on Unsplash

I enjoy watching golf. The game is quite simple. **The low score**

wins.

Golfers have their scorecards. It records their strokes on each hole.

Wouldn't it be nice if there was a scorecard for developers? *Software development is more complex.* Some things we want less of, like bugs. Others we want more of completed tasks.

Developer Scorecard

What would you put in a developer scorecard? There are quite a few I could think of. For instance, we would want specific technical skills. As well as interpersonal skills too.

Technical

As a developer, we expect a baseline in technical skills. Imagine that you are a Java developer. You should have a basic under-standing of Java.

Along with that, we should have some ancillary skills too. You should know how to use GitHub. Or some other code repository.

Team

Coding is increasingly more collaborative. Teams code and create together more and more. Even if you are a big introvert you need to cooperate with others.

Collaboration

It's common to come across people with inflated egos, even among developers. However, to foster collaboration, it's crucial to set aside our egos.

It's important to remember that good ideas can come from anyone, and no one person or group has exclusive ownership over them. Share yours and help improve others. Credit should go to the team. Coding is a team sport.

Guiding

When a new person joins the team, help guide them into the codebase. Share insights and learnings.

Pairing

How well do you pair? Can you take suggestions from a junior developer? That is one I have worked on. Originally I would have let my pride get in the way.

Individual

I would put the team first. Of course, we need to evaluate each member too. How are they contributing? We are looking for collaborators not, lone wolves.

Quality

How can we determine if the developer produces quality code? One way is to identify any defects in the code.

Another question is do your automated tests pass? Does the Quality Assurance team like testing your code?

Through my many coding mistakes, I have learned how to get the Product Owner's input. As well as talk to your Quality engineer too. See how they would test it.

Commits

How often do they commit? I am a firm believer in committing often. Similar to being out past midnight, large commits infrequently lead to trouble.

User Stories

I know the user story we get might not be perfect. Apply the Boy Scout rule to your story. **Leave it better than you found it.**

Don't complain endlessly about incomplete stories. Ask lots of questions and clean it up.

Regardless of what you put in your developer scorecard make sure it helps you evaluate your team. This would be good to align with a team agreement.

I have spoken before about coding heroes. Make sure you foster a team that works together. What you accept can create a good team or a bad team. It is up to you.

10

How to get Business Analysts and Developers to row in the same direction

Photo by RUN 4 FFWPU:
https://www.pexels.com/photo/man-rowing-boat-3554634/

"Why won't my developers work with me?" Asked Padma who was in the audience from a virtual presentation to an IIBA

Chapter. "I wish I had a quick answer, Padma. Let me ask you a few questions first." I responded.

Padma's question is quite common. I have presented Humans are Hard, Code is Easy to multiple IIBA Chapters. Let's recap the questions I asked her and a few options you can consider.

5 Questions for Clarity

1. **What is your current state?** Find out what is happening now. Try to understand what they are seeing.
2. **Define what working together means to you.** Give them details of your expectations. Perhaps they want the developer to tell them everything. If they are quiet this can be challenging.
3. **What are the roadblocks you are experiencing?** Are there organizational issues in place? For instance, how the team is organized may limit our influence.
4. **What can you control?** Focus on what levers you have. If there are things outside of your control don't spend too much time on them. Where do you have agency? Understand your *sphere of influence*.
5. **How can you iterate to a solution?** Learn from our agile friends. Find ways to make small experiments. Gain feedback. Adjust your approach. Small hinges swing big doors.

4 Options for Better Collaboration

Train

Collaboration is a bit squishy. Like Justice Potter Stewart's quote about pornography, "I know it when I see it." Train your team in the basics of collaboration.

Model the behavior you want. This will give everyone an example of what collaboration looks like.

Keep curious. Ask the team members how they would handle things. Get them to share.

Foster group problem-solving. Instill in them the best way forward is together. No lone wolf approaches.

Access

To work well together everyone needs access to the information. On one team only the Business Analyst could talk to the stakeholder. The developers had to communicate through her.

This limited the developers' access and information. Free flow of information to the team is critical to their success. **This is the lifeblood for meeting goals.**

Check-In

Having been a leader in the past, you can believe things are going well. Until you begin asking a few questions. *Dig in and see how the collaboration is going.*

As a developer myself, I know we can be hard to work with. We may not always communicate clearly. Therefore, Business Analysts might think we are mad. In reality, we can be introverted.

Communicate

Collaboration doesn't happen in a vacuum. Two or more people need to work together. Along with the previous point, we need to communicate our intent. "I plan on completing this requirement by the end of the day."

If that plan changes we need to let everyone know. In our remote world, some people call this "Working out Loud". For instance, we post in Slack or Teams and note this in Jira as well. Make sure people know what you are working on.

Achieving alignment can be hard work. Building cohesion on the team is worth it. Be clear and direct with them.

11

Why you need to try Value Stream Mapping

As I continue to learn more about DevOps and Agile development I hear a lot of influencers talk about Value Stream Mapping. Asking many experts and doing a little research has helped me understand how powerful this can be. However, this can be a great tool to use in your initial assessment of any transformation.

As a newbie to the DevOps world, I like how value stream mapping gives you the ability to assess where you are. Therefore, anytime I start something be it a new job, coaching engagement, or consulting opportunity I think it is important to start to know exactly where we are.

What?

Wikipedia defines it as "Value stream mapping is a lean management tool that helps visualize the steps needed to take from product creation to delivering it to the end-customer. As with other business process mapping methods, it helps with introspection (understanding your business better), as well as analysis and process improvement." In other words, this is a great tool to help assess the current process.

Why?

Many agile practitioners encourage us to make work visible. Value Stream Mapping can help get everyone on the same page and see the process through its entirety. In addition, Lean management teaches us to eliminate waste in our process.

How?

Great so how do I get started? Sonia Pearson from Tallify shares 7 steps to Value Stream Mapping.

1. Decide how far you want to go
2. Define the steps
3. Indicate the information flows
4. Gather the critical data
5. Add data and timelines to the map
6. Identify the 7 wastes of Lean
7. Create the ideal Value Stream Map

These basic steps should get you going in the right direction.

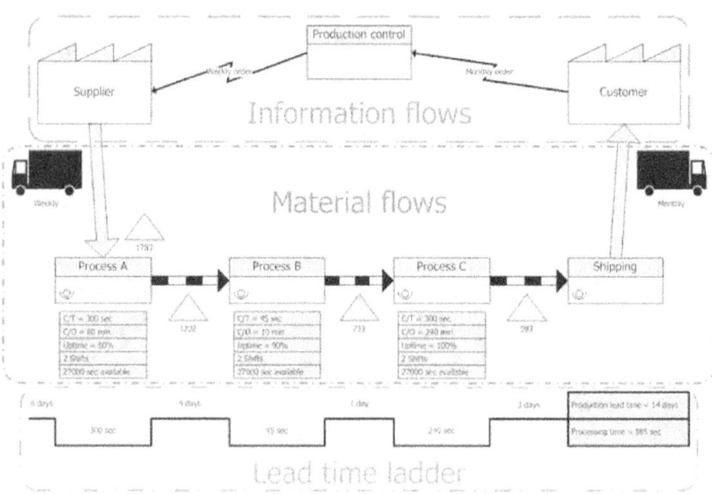

Value Stream Mapping from Wikimedia Commons

Sections

As you can see in this example there are three different parts to the Value Stream Map. Plutora shares with us some nice descriptions of all three.

Information — This section shows the communication of process-related information and the transmission of data.

Product — This section maps the steps of the development lifecycle from concept to delivery.

Time — The Time Ladder provides a somewhat simplistic visual representation of the value stream timeline.

When?

There are differing opinions on how often and when to use a Value Stream Map. Above all, it helps to take a step back and see what our goal is. Similarly, I found this to be sage advice. "As with all lean improvement projects, you should **first have a problem that you want to fix!** Then, depending on the problem, you collect data, make different analyses, and use appropriate lean tools to improve your problem."

In conclusion, we shared some basics about the power of Value Stream Mapping. From how to when. Just remember to make sure you have your problem well-defined. Otherwise, you are wasting time. Using Lean Principles we want to eliminate waste not add to it!

How could you use Value Stream Mapping in your work?

12

Uncovering the simple waste here in IT

Waste is prevalent in many technology departments. Our friends in Lean Manufacturing have eight different types of waste. We can focus on three types that hit IT hard.

Recently I re-read Eliyahu Goldratt's classic The Goal. It reminded me why Brandon Carlson suggested I read this years ago. There is so much good advice that we need to come back and remember.

The story in The Goal deals with a fictitious manufacturing plant. Where the manager runs into an old college professor who has some sage advice for him. He reveals to him how to find much of the waste in his system.

Waste

To define what waste is we can turn to this article that does it quite well.

> "Waste is any step or action in a process that is not required to complete a process (called "Non Value-Adding") successfully. When Waste is removed, only the steps that are required (called "Value-Adding") to deliver a satisfactory product or service to the customer remain in the process."

That defines it succinctly.

Defects

I am a software developer and I create my fair share of defects. Although I can't say they were all my fault. Some of course were but, occasionally we have miscommunication with our stakeholders. Either way, we still are creating waste.

Defects create the need for rework no matter who was at fault. Perhaps we need to scrap the work as it can't be completed on time or within the allotted budget. This is a common form of waste in many technology departments.

Overproduction

The Goal hits on a big form of waste called overproduction. In corporations, I see this with the *"Silo-thinking"* that prevails. For instance, let's say we have a department of Business Analysts. They efficiently create requirements.

What is wrong with that? you say. The problem is when you have defined more work than your team of developers can do in a few months. This is a big waste of time and chances are your stakeholders will change their minds or de-prioritize this work.

In Goldratt's Theory of Constraints, this is known as a *"local optimization"*. The Business Analysts are working in efficient batches for them but not for the rest of the delivery team.

Inventory

Starting something new before you have completed the previous item is a big "no-no". I know this logically but, fail to live it from time to time. Lean reminds us that if we start 100 things in one week but only finish 10 we are creating waste.

Sure you say we will get to it later. We can do this when we buy a Costco-size bag of chips. It seems like a good deal to buy this huge bag. Of course, later on, when you eat them and they are stale you waste that supposed savings.

Limit your Work In Progress. The batch size needs to be optimized for what you can complete. You may think you need to be busy all the time. In The Goal, we learned how this can guide us in the wrong direction.

Where do you see the waste in your department?

13

How to craft better code using OOP Principles

We have covered some basic principles in object-oriented programming. Abstraction, Composition, Encapsulation, and Polymorphism are important concepts to master. Let's review some key principles that will help you craft better code.

In college, I tried to learn Tae Kwon Do. I was quite clumsy at first and could not get the moves down. After sticking with it for a while I began to advance in ranks a little.

Tae Kwon Do teaches some principles in the forms you learn. As a white belt, I had a form to practice that involved very basic moves. Each step up I encountered new moves to learn.

The coding craftsman needs to master and keep these principles in mind as they develop their solutions.

DRY

I first learned about DRY or Don't Repeat Yourself in the Pragmatic Programmer. They define it as, "every piece of knowledge must have a single, unambiguous, authoritative representation within a system".

This simple principle is violated all the time. We copy some code instead of calling it. I am just as guilty as the next person.

Working on your next assignment takes a little more time to review the codebase. Is there a similar solution you could use? Perhaps some slight refactoring can make some code used for multiple items.

Single Responsibility

I enjoy looking at tools at the hardware store. I may not be able to use them all but they are nice and shiny. Some can do so many things. However, when they do that, they don't work so well.

Software developers have a principle of single responsibility. Unlike these multi-function tools that perform poorly, we want our code to do one thing.

Severin Perez describes it like this, "The single responsibility principle (SRP) states that every class or module in a program should have responsibility for just a single piece of that program's functionality."

Open Closed Design

When you achieve a great design you don't have to make changes. I strive for that in my work but, rarely accomplish that feat.

The Open Closed Design principle inspires us to push for that goal. As Joel Abrahamsson states, "We should strive to write code that doesn't have to be changed every time the requirements change."

Create a solution that is open for extension and closed for modification. In Java, we want to utilize interfaces. Favor interfaces over the use of subclassing.

Even after almost twenty years of developing software, I find it good to remind myself of these principles. We can all violate these from time to time in our haste to meet a deadline.

How do you keep your code from repeating?

What checks do you use to make sure your code has a single responsibility?

14

Building Your Personal Brand

The keys to brand success are self-definition, trans-parency, authenticity, and accountability.
Simon Mainwaring

We each have a personal brand. Some of us work on building it while others may just let it happen. It helps to be conscious of the parts that make up your brand. Most of my technology friends may ignore this fact. To stand out though you want to work at making an exceptional brand.

Authenticity

Never try to be someone you are not. As you build your brand make sure it is authentic. Oscar Wilde said, "Be yourself; everyone else is already taken." So while you may want to imitate some famous tech titan, it is best to be yourself.

Performance

Recently we tried a new restaurant. We were quite impressed with the people working there and the food. A few weeks later we decided to come back. The next visit was completely different. It was busy and the quality was poor. Just like with a restaurant how you perform is part of your brand. Focus on making it a good thing. Take pride in the work you do day after day. The hallmark of a true professional is doing a good job day in and day out.

Linkedin

Technology people tend to move around more than many other industries. This makes something like a LinkedIn profile important. Essentially it starts with your online resume for a profile. Then you can add your connections and recommendations. Of course, some people avoid it as many recruiters will contact you.

This is not always a bad thing. They can be helpful when you are looking for a new opportunity.

Community

It always is helpful to be part of the community. Technology communities can be quite tight-knit ones. Working in Des Moines for almost twenty years I am always amazed at the strong community. Even though Des Moines is not a major market, we have many strong technology groups. Our local .Net Group and Agile Iowa are quite strong. Each has yearly conferences that draw huge crowds. One great way to build your brand is to get involved with your local community.

Participation

A few years ago I got involved in a group. I reluctantly began to be an officer in the group. Looking back it was a great opportunity to participate and give back. I helped the group grow and transition. We all think we are too busy to be involved. I would recommend trying it out. You will learn more than you can imagine. Plus you may find something that you are good at in the process.

Permission

Building your brand means you. Don't create a brand by copying someone you don't have permission to copy. This happens online when people see a great design for something and decide to copy it. Also, organizations have guidelines on what you can share and how you can share it. For instance, if your company is acquiring another that is probably not something you have permission to share.

Just Ask...

One great way to understand your brand is to ask other people. Ask them what they think your brand is. You might find some interesting responses. If you don't like what you hear perhaps you have some work to do. Find others who have a stronger brand. Look at how they created the brand and there may be some lessons there.

15

XML the Language of data

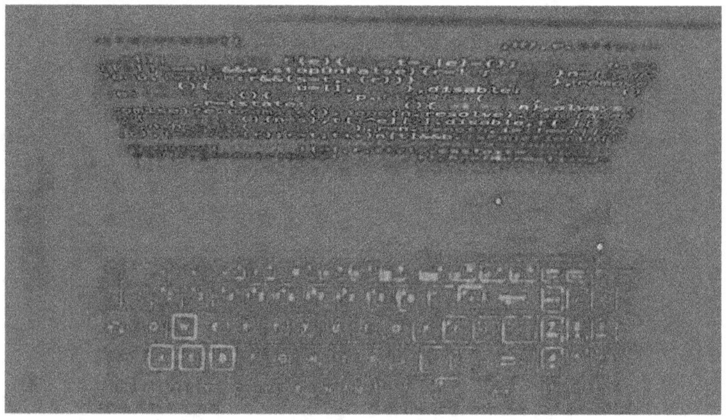

We have spoken a little bit about XML before along with JSON. Today let's go deeper and focus on what XML data is used for and how it came about. As a bonus, I will give you a cheesy example too.

I have a confession to make. When I was a teenager I would curse a lot. I thought it was a way to make myself sound mature. After a few years of doing this, a teacher pointed out how it wasn't having the intended outcome. Therefore, he shared how it reflected poor intelligence and vocabulary. He thought that wasn't the image I wanted to portray.

Language is truly a reflection of ourselves. When we work with lots of data one language you will no doubt run into is XML. XML has been around for a while and I have run into it many times in different incarnations. Like any technology, it has changed over time and been used in different fashions.

What is XML?

According to W3Schools "XML stands for eXtensible Markup Language" and "a markup language much like HTML". So that doesn't tell us much. It was meant to be used to store and transport data. As you look at it you can see how that is at the heart of what it is for. However, HTML does not have to worry about aesthetics. Although humans should be able to easily decipher what data it carries. Sometimes it falls short of that goal. I don't think my mom is going to look over my XML...

Why Do We Need XML?

It does seem like there are other data formats out there. So why do we need XML? When we need to display data to many formats it helps to have XML as a means we can use to pass the data around and then use formatting to make it render in a way we can easily use or read. It can also be passed from web services to update and share information.

XML Data Example

Well, we have talked enough about XML let's take a look and see it. Let's create an email XML that we can all understand.

```
<Email>
<To>Santa</To>
<From>Little Johnny</From>
<Subject>Better presents</Subject>
Santa,
My sister Debbie has been getting better presents for
two years now.
Please step up your game!
Thanks,
Little Johnnie
</Body>
</Email>
```

Note how our example has an opening tag and a closing tag for each element. We need to mark the start and end of each element. As you can see our body starts with an open tag. In addition, we close it with the closing tag which is quite similar to the open just one extra character. There is a hierarchy in this example which is typical of XML. So we need to have the email tag first. Then we can nest the additional tags.

If you want open XML you can use most text editors. Also, your typical programming IDE can handle them and perhaps give you some validation too. This can be helpful for newbies. You may forget to close your tags properly.

XML Data History

From the very start, XML was created to make the internet usable. There was a team that came together to do this. They used SGML as a foundation to start in 1996. In addition, this helped jumpstart the goal instead of starting from scratch. Within the first five months, a working copy was released. Version 1.0 of XML was approved by W3 in 1998.

In conclusion, XML is a valuable tool to have in your toolbox. Even if you don't use it every day you now understand what it is and why we need it. The example helped you understand the basics. We covered the basic history. Where do you go next? That depends on what you need from it. Perhaps this is enough for you. Dig deeper if that fits you.

What have you used XML for?

16

Why don't the developers speak up? The secrets to engaging the whole team

Photo by Antony Trivet: https://www.pexels.com/photo/people-standing-and-having-a-conversation-12970978/

Have you ever dreamt of a meeting where everyone is engaged? The Stakeholders, the Quality Assurance, and the developers? How come this rarely happens?

Let's review how to find your voice and help others do the same. Perhaps you are presenting at an upcoming event. Don't wing it. Have a plan.

Speaking

When you see a great speaker they make it look easy. Of course, if it were we could all be professionals. Unfortunately, much like woodworking, it is more complicated than it looks. Although in speaking we usually don't cut off a finger...

Know your audience

If you want to get better at speaking join Toastmasters. They teach you a lot. One of the first things is to **know your audience.**

Who are they? What do they want out of this? For instance, if you are meeting with other developers you would focus on different things than if you were talking to a group of leaders.

Warm-up

As a software developer, I don't talk a lot throughout the day. When I get ready to speak to an audience I need to warm up my voice. Perhaps this sounds strange to you.

Have you ever played an instrument? If you don't warm up and tune your instrument it can sound awful. Instead of being pleasant, it can be downright awful. Here are a few ways to warm up.

Ums and ahs

In Toastmasters, they have an "Um counter" in every meeting. This person listens for "ums" and "ahs". If you have never been it can be eye-popping.

The first time I spoke there I wasn't aware of this. These really detract from your message. *Cleaning these up can be a game-changer!*

Plan

Earlier in my speaking career, I would try to wing a talk. Essentially get up without a plan. The results were subpar.

A few years ago I was fortunate to attend Heroic Public Speaking. Michael Port author of *Steal the Show* trains you to give better speeches. A major part of a successful speech is **preparation**.

Learn from my mistakes. Before you open your mouth have a plan. **Even in a meeting.** Don't just open your mouth and start yapping!

Story

Why do we remember some things and forget others? Dan and Chip Heath explore this in Made to Stick. One reason is a compelling story.

The Heath brothers insist we stop marketing and tell stories. *They outline how ideas are stickier that way.*

One way to do this is to **challenge** your audience. For instance, the story of David vs Goliath describes a challenge. David faces the giant and wins.

Succinct

Do you know Karl? He comes to my meetings and talks. And talks. Although he really never says anything. He sounds like the teacher from Charlie Brown. *"Wah wah woh wah wah"*

> Law 4: Always Say Less Than Necessary -*48 Laws of Power* by Robert Greene

Be **succinct** in your message. From Merriam-Webster, "marked by compact precise expression without wasted words." In other words, say your piece and shut up.

Presenting your case

When you have to present something you want to make sure your case is airtight. As we walked through before, first know your audience. Create a plan of what to say.

Next review if it is succinct. Don't waste people's time. Talk through it with a trusted friend. Make sure they give you honest feedback. Then rehearse your points.

Practice

Here are a few ways to practice your speaking.

Um counting

Pair up with a friend. Try to introduce yourself by talking for only 60 seconds. Have your friend count any "ums" and "ahs". You might be stunned.

Know your audience

You need to communicate a change in scope. Discuss with your partner how to deliver the message differently to Project Managers, Scrum Master, Business Analysts, or a developer.

Roleplay

You need to communicate a change in deadlines to the team. Role-play with your partner on how you would share that. Have the partner become angry. Try to respond calmly.

17

Code smells from mild to Strong

Code smells are something all developers deal with. We want to make sure you are aware of them. Let's learn what they are and how to stop them.

> If Stupidity got us into this mess, then why can't it get us out?

Will Rogers

I can remember some of the earliest Java code I wrote. It was pretty gnarly stuff. Once someone mentioned code smells and I read a little bit I knew I was a major violator!

Code Smells

According to Wikipedia a Code Smell is:

> In computer programming, a code smell is any characteristic in the source code of a program that possibly indicates a deeper problem.

This article details some of the basic code smells. I would assume at one time or another I have made all of these mistakes.

Bloaters

Cory was a character that I worked with many years ago. He liked to poke fun at mistakes others had made. There was one class that had been touched by many hands and grown to the size of a novel. He printed out the file and taped it together outside of his cube. It got people's attention but he didn't win many friends. This was an example of a "Bloater". We start with good intentions and then someone adds a few lines here and there. Soon it has grown too big! This can be a large class or a super long method.

OO Abusers

The Java language has the switch statement. Object-oriented design is usually a sign of lazy design. It is better to remove it and create a method to handle this. Another option is to replace the type code with the subclass. This can be a great place to use polymorphism to handle the changes.

Change Preventers

One of my first duties as a professional developer was to make changes to an order entry system. The original developer had made most tasks flow through one very large program. It was so unwieldy that the person who was guiding at the time said don't touch that main program. It was so large it was a change preventer. Everyone was scared to touch anything for the fact of what might happen.

Dispensable

If you have ever seen an episode of the A&E Network show Hoarders you will understand what dispensables are in code. Programmers can be reluctant to delete code. Think of this as a digital packrat! When a feature is no longer used we need to delete it, not keep it around like artwork.

Couplers

My wife likes to watch the Bachelor on ADC. They have a formula of ladies who get intimate with the Bachelor and then cause drama among the contestants. If your classes need to share too much information, it might be time to refactor. Come on keep it professional, please.

Every developer spends a lot of time on <u>Stackoverflow.com</u>. One of the founders Jeff Atwood who occasionally blogs at CodingHorror shared some good recommendations on code smells.

Comments

Jeff brings up some great questions regarding comments. I see this in many codebases. Some refactoring could eliminate the need for some comments.

Long Method

We touched on this before but it bears repeating. Methods need to be succinct and to the point. Name your method something and just do that! Please don't add a few other things it is probably best to create a new one instead.

Duplicated Code

This is a personal favorite of mine. I worked at a company once that had the same method in 142 different places in the same codebase. I was blown away! Put it in one place and Don't Repeat Yourself! (aka DRY principle)

So if you are a coder you should be aware of the issues that code smells indicate. There may be times when you can knowingly violate one of these. Of course, be careful what mess you leave behind for our fellow developers.

18

Build your brand like Linus with a bit of marketing insight

Photo by Tom Swinnen: https://www.pexels.com/photo/close-up-photography-of-apple-computer-1034649/

One of the biggest things developers can do to stand out doesn't have anything to do with coding.

What do Linus Torvalds, Dave Farley, and Javier Lozano have in common? Keep reading to find out.

Branding

We all admire certain brands. Perhaps you are an Apple fan. Or maybe every day you trek to Starbucks.

Ok, Tom, this is going a little far. What does branding have to do with software development?

I thought the same thing. Then I began to look around. I noticed that the leaders in the coding arena had this. *They built a brand that set them apart.*

Examples

Here are three examples we can use.

Linus Torvalds creator of Linux and Git.

Javier Lozano member of .Net Foundation.

Dave Farley co-author of Continuous Delivery.

Create

Each one of these has created a brand for themselves. Linus is probably the most popular. Many of us use Linux and Git every day.

Regardless they have crafted a brand. This brand focuses their work. Instead of learning lots of different things, they said "no".

The act of focusing helped them become noteworthy. Using Cal Newport's term they have put in **Deep Work.**

Share

Each of these three shares in their own way. Linus creates and shares his open-source software. Many of us use Git every day.

Javier is a Microsoft MVP. This is an award for those who share expertise with the community. He has repeatedly earned this award by presenting and helping others learn.

Dave Farley has been a thought leader for some time. First, the book he co-authored with Jez Humble. Now with his YouTube Channel.

Consistent

Branding has to be consistent. We can't be all over the map. For instance, Javier is all about .Net. He doesn't vacillate.

Southwest Airlines is focused on being a low-cost airline. This helps them filter decisions—no frills just low prices.

Specialize

These three examples specialize. They are not generalists. The focus helps them create a unique brand.

My guess is you have gotten conflicting advice on this. I have too. Although the people that stand out specialize.

Correct

Be on the lookout for feedback. If your brand isn't working adjust it. Ask your peers.

A few years ago Novell networks were big. Today they essentially don't exist. Always be looking out for trends.

Change

Having a brand means it must adapt. We need to make subtle changes as we go. As Linux grew Linus had to shift their focus.

Developers can get stuck in our ways. Although the pace of change in technology can leave us behind. Keep moving forward.

With these suggestions in mind, How can you apply them to your developer career? What would someone you work with say is your brand? Whether you admit it or not you have one.

You can disregard this and keep on trucking. Or you can reassess where you are and think about what supports your brand. It could be you just need a subtle shift.

On the other hand, you may need to start a complete overhaul. A former leader of mine was once deemed "The Elvis of Clipper." What is Clipper you ask? I didn't know either.

Technology work is a tumultuous sea. We need to make sure we stay on the right ship. If things are trending down. It may be time to jump ship. (Okay Tom enough with the sailing metaphors...)

Take a step back and look at your career. Better to change your brand than to neglect it. You will regret it later if you do!

19

Leaner and Meaner: Lean Development

"The most dangerous kind of waste is the waste we do not recognize."
  Shigeo Shingo

Have you ever wondered why some organizations can be so wasteful? As a high school student, a friend of mine's uncle was a truck driver. He would tell stories about goods that seemed fine but could not be sold for one reason or the other. These goods were given to the truck driver or sent to the trash. Having grandparents that lived through the Depression I saw them waste hardly a thing. Lean manufacturing focuses on reducing waste and lean development does the same. Let's start by reviewing some principles.

Principles

If you search around for Lean Development on the internet most resources point back to one book. Implementing Lean Software Development by Mary and Tom Poppendieck is a seminal work. In it, they outline the key principles of Lean Development. Let's review the seven they discuss here.

Eliminate Waste

Waste is anything that gets in the way of delivering value to the customer. Partially complete code is a form of waste. You see the emphasis on shipping code in the Scrum model. Churn or changing requirements is a form of waste. This is a waste of developers' time and yields no value for the customer. Requirements gathering way ahead of time and testing long after the code has been written are also wasteful. Integration delays are wasteful and can cause delays. For this purpose, many organizations use continuous integration.

Build in Quality

Poppendieck's point out that defects are in essence incomplete work. If we use measures to prevent defects early like Continuous Integration and Test-Driven Development(TDD) we can eliminate many defects. The earlier the defect is found the more money is saved and value delivered. Lean principles focus on the system. Some managers will browbeat developers who create defects. Lean says the system is part of the problem. Expect to change your code and refactor it often. Create programs that are easily changed.

Create Knowledge

We must create software that can evolve. Don't expect it to correct the first time. Do builds daily to get feedback on your changes. Share your learning with your team and organization. Build learning into the system, therefore, everyone can learn. Don't waste your learning or your organization will regret it.

Defer Commitment

I was having a conversation with Tim Gifford from Lean Techniques once. He brought this up and it was hard for me to understand right away. Having a plan mapped out can be reassuring. As I have learned more about lean though I understand why this helps. Deciding too early can cause waste. Also, making decisions reversible can help us back out of something that seems not to work. Now I just need to work on my wife who plans out our trips two years in advance...

Deliver fast

The faster we can deliver value we can get compensated for our work. Half-done software isn't worth much to anyone. Look for ways to streamline your process. Along with this seek out opportunities to eliminate defects as well. Simple things like using Test Driven Development can't find issues early before they get out in the wild.

Respect People

We need to be reminded of the importance of showing appreciation for our people. Don't take them for granted. Leaders need to show each team member respect for their contribution. The example leaders set is the most important thing they do. For instance, if they let a high performer get away with treating teammates they have set an example. Make sure your actions impart respect for the team and organization.

Optimize the Whole

Reading The Goal by Eli Goldratt teaches us not to optimize for parts but the whole system. This is an important lesson we need to learn and be reminded of again and again. Managers can obsess about people being busy. I have never met a manager who was incentivized to keep people busy.

Pros and Cons

Let's quickly review some pros and cons of Lean Development. First, we can start with the pros.

Reduce time wasters

Everyone wastes time. As a big fan of <u>Michael Hyatt,</u> I am amazed at how he can see new ways to be more effective. He seems to share productivity tips constantly. Thinking Lean we can always review our processes and find more efficient ways to do things. What are you doing now that you could stop?

Save Money

When lean thinking reduces waste it saves money. By completing the right work we can provide value. Forget the ten different things to work on have your team focus and save money not working on the features no one cares about.

Need a good team

The first con is that it requires a good team. I wish that all teams were good but, we know that is not the case. I am sure you like me have been on a good team and a few bad teams. When a team works well together they can do amazing things. Sad to say that doesn't happen too often. Lean works best with a good team. Lean principles can't save a bad team. Of course, there isn't much that can.

Documentation

It never says in the Agile Manifesto that we should never document anything. If it helps we should do it. Lean principles require a team to document some things so they can repeatedly achieve their goals. Overall Lean principles can be helpful but you need to understand these cons too.

20

How to onboard developers successfully

Let's forget the baggage of the past and make a new
beginning.
Shehbaz Sharif

Each time we start a new developer we need to make a conscious decision to bring them in and make them feel welcomed. I have had many experiences of being a new person. Each company does this differently. Some make you feel welcomed others make you feel like you are unwanted. Therefore with a little time and a checklist, you can successfully onboard a new developer.

Hiring

You might think that hiring is too early to be thinking about onboarding but, you would be wrong. On the Codementor blog they correctly point out that, "Hiring may not typically be considered onboarding, but it is the requisite step. Get the hiring wrong and your onboarding won't matter much." Mess this up and you set a bad precedent for your new teammates.

Pre-onboarding

Pre-onboarding, what does that mean? I have seen some major snafus when bringing new people on board. However, when you get pre-onboarding you make sure everything is ready. Ilie Ghiciuc shares on the Usersnap blog, "A lot of the pre-onboarding tasks are done behind the scenes before the new developer comes on board. We try to make sure to have all the hardware available, all the software tools they need, and if they are on-site employees, we give them access to the building."

Documentation

A famous bard once wrote, "Brevity is the soul of wit". In a similar fashion that is how I like my documentation. Straight to the point and of course up to date. When someone new comes in for their first day you want them to have documentation that they can glean the basics from quickly.

Mentor

Developers get a bad rap for having little if any people skills. They still need a mentor to help them get through the things you won't document but forgot you learned the first few days. Also, it might not hurt to pair program with them and show them around the codebase.

Don't forget this if you have remote employees. Mentoring is still possible. You can easily use things like Zoom to discuss things face-to-face and mentor new remote employees.

Setup

The first day is stressful enough that you don't need to add insult to injury and not have things ready. It should go without saying to have their computer ready. Of course, I know that many places still mess that up!

Along with the hardware don't forget about the proper software they will need. Yes, they may want to install a few extra things but get them the basics and any access they need. Don't make them have to grovel to the help desk people in the first week for access to all the systems. Create a checklist for this and make sure you have it ready!

Culture

Great writing culture is hard to describe but, you know it when you see it. As I have worked at many companies I see how every company has a culture. Of course, some are created with a purpose while others have a culture by accident. Every part of the onboarding process needs to reinforce the company culture. It is not one thing you check off the list. Take a step back and think about your culture. How do you try to share it when you onboard new folks? If you don't know you are probably creating a culture accident.

Communication

How does your company communicate? This basic question can tell you a lot. Some more modern companies might do everything in Slack. Whereas the more conservative companies still live in email. Let people know how to talk to their teammates. Remote teams have to pay attention to these methods. Honor people's time differences and life situations. It can be helpful to post normal hours in chat so your teammate in Europe can let you sleep.

Coding

Developers code. Let's help them out and discuss how coding works at the new company. Do you have any coding standards? If so these should be explained. Do you have continuous integration? You should discuss the process that you use. Make the expectations explicit. It should not be a gotcha game where we berate the developer in their first code review.

Development Plan

Software is constantly changing. Developers should have a plan for the skills they want to pursue. This can be quite basic as they want to learn node.js. Or it could be a longer more detailed plan. I find it helpful to have new skills to learn along with foundational skills that we should enhance.

As you review this article I hope you come away with some basics. Overall it is important to have a plan when you bring in a new software developer. Don't let things happen by accident. More than likely if that is the case it will be a bad experience and they will want to leave.

How do you, onboard new developers?

21

First 100 days for a developer

Photo by Markus Spiske: https://www.pexels.com/photo/codes-on-tilt-shift-lens-2004161/

A new job. How exciting!

Learning new things. Meeting new people.

Although we need to start things out right.

If you don't do these in your first 100 days it could be disastrous.

Gratitude

Nothing is a bigger turn-off than entitlement. I once worked for a company that had the team take the new employee out to lunch on the first day.

As we sat down for lunch the new employee started complaining.

Wow! I thought to myself. This is how you want to start. The team was taken aback.

She was making a bad impression on the team. The sad part about this is she was let go a few months later. *It was not a good fit.*

When you start something new begin with gratitude. Entitlement is never a helpful emotion.

Clarify

Start out on the right foot. Find clear expectations with your new leader. How do they expect work to be completed?

Are there team agreements? Are they followed? These can help you understand how the team works. Or perhaps doesn't work.

Use the newbie card. **Ask a lot of questions.** See who is willing to share. Others may be annoyed. That is important to know.

Tech

Developers may want to start here. We need to have the previous two in place. Then we can clear this up.

What is the technical stack? You should know most of this from the interview. Although you have missed something.

Do I need to study something? For instance, I have a long history with Java development. In my current role, I needed to learn AWS and Vue.js.

With this in mind, I created a learning plan to brush up on these. I wrote about my learning for AWS here.

Connect

Get to know your teammates. Learn their names. Ask where they are from. Understand their strengths.

Each of us tends to specialize. Keep this in mind. This will come in handy as you run into challenges.

A great way to connect is to Pair or Mob. You get to know your teammates. They can share their knowledge.

Plus you will learn some new techniques. They may use a tool you have never used. Learning is always good for your career.

Feedback

Seek feedback. Similar to the earlier point on clarifying. This is focused on you.

How am I doing? What should I be doing that I am not? A few questions to consider.

We all have blind spots. See what others say. Remember you can take it or leave it.

Fit

Lastly, we want to ensure this is a good fit. Do you feel your work is good for you? There are many factors.

If things aren't a good fit that is not the end of the world. First, determine where things are out of alignment. Next, have discussions with your leader and team.

This doesn't mean you have to leave. You just started this new job. Take time to make things right.

It may be as little as changing some responsibilities. Or having an in-depth conversation with the team.

For instance, if one person works long hours that doesn't necessarily mean you need to. Be firm from the start.

On the whole, we want to start right. Have open conversations. Understand what is expected technically and from the team.

Become part of the team. Prompt others for feedback. Make sure it works for you. Then you are off to good things.

About the Author

Tom Henricksen is a problem-solving technology professional. He is a speaker and writer at Code is Easy. Starting from a developer he has worked as a Project Manager, Technical Lead, Scrum Master, and Manager of Software Development.

Tom has helped organizations with agile transformations. He has also coached and trained teams and individuals.

Tom has been an entrepreneur as well. He speaks and writes with a focus on technology roles. Tom was the founder of the Agile Online Summit and DevOps Online Summit. Where he led a strong online community of over 5,000 people.

Tom has learned how to solve challenging issues in technology and lead technical teams. He can help you develop those skills too!

You can connect with me on:

🌐 http://codeiseasy.co

🐦 https://twitter.com/TomHenricksen

🔗 https://www.linkedin.com/in/tomhenricksen

Subscribe to my newsletter:

✉ https://t.co/NkolrQgXHM